PRESENTED TO:

_____

FROM:

_____

DATE:

_____

YOUR
Best Life
NOW
for Moms

JOEL OSTEEN

New York Boston Nashville

Literary development and design: Koechel Peterson & Associates, Inc., Minneapolis, Minnesota.

Portions of this book have been adapted from *Your Best Life Now*, copyright © 2004 and *Daily Readings from Your Best Life Now*, copyright © 2005 by Joel Osteen. Published by FaithWords.

FaithWords
Hachette Book Group USA
237 Park Avenue, New York, NY 10169
Visit our Web site at www.faithwords.com.

The FaithWords name and logo are trademarks of Hachette Book Group, USA.

Printed in the United States of America.
First Printing: April 2007
10 9 8 7 6 5 4 3 2 1
ISBN: 0-446-58100-3
ISBN-13: 978-0-446-58100-4
Library of Congress Control Number: 2006936801

TABLE OF CONTENTS

MOTHER IS THE NAME FOR GOD IN THE LIPS

AND HEARTS OF LITTLE CHILDREN.

–WILLIAM MAKEPEACE THACKERY

Introduction

THE PROVERBS 31 LADY IS EXTRAORDINARY in every facet of her life. She is the perfect wife and the ideal mother wrapped up in one person. One cannot read the descriptions of her noble character and not want everything that she is and has.

Yet we all know that while some moms grab life with enthusiasm and find great joy in motherhood, such a grandiose dream doesn't always pan out for everybody. I'm not talking about becoming a perfect mother. I recognize the strain of nighttime feedings and chicken pox and toilet training and temper tantrums and personality differences and on and on. No mom is perfect, and not every moment is glorious. Motherhood has its ups and downs and tremendous challenges.

But I am talking about moms who never seem to get even close to discovering the joy of motherhood. Why is that? What makes the difference?

Happy, successful, fulfilled moms have learned how to live their best lives *now*. They make the most of the present moment and thereby enhance their future. You can, too. No matter where you are or what challenges you face, you can enjoy your life right now!

Many women enter motherhood with low self-esteem, focusing on the negative, feeling inferior or inadequate, always dwelling on reasons why they can't be happy. Others put off their happiness till some future date. Unfortunately, "someday" never comes. Today is the only day we have. We can't do anything about the past, and we don't know what the future holds. ***But we can live at our full potential right now!***

In this book, you will discover just how to do that. Within these pages, you will find seven simple, yet profound, steps to improve your life as a mom. If you take these steps, you ultimately will be happier than ever before, living with joy, peace, and enthusiasm for the rest of your life!

I challenge you to break out of the "barely-get-by" mentality that possesses so many moms, to become the best you can be, not merely average or ordinary. To do that, you may have to rid yourself of some negative mind-sets that are holding you back and start seeing yourself as doing more, enjoying more, being more. That is what it means to live your best life now!

SHE IS CLOTHED WITH STRENGTH AND DIGNITY;

SHE CAN LAUGH AT THE DAYS TO COME.

SHE SPEAKS WITH WISDOM,

AND FAITHFUL INSTRUCTION IS ON HER TONGUE.

SHE WATCHES OVER THE AFFAIRS OF HER HOUSEHOLD

AND DOES NOT EAT THE BREAD OF IDLENESS.

HER CHILDREN ARISE AND CALL HER BLESSED.

—THE BOOK OF PROVERBS

ENLARGE
Your Vision

As a mom, you serve the Most High God,

and His dream for your life

and for your family

is so much bigger and better

than you can even imagine.

MOTHERHOOD IS PRICED OF GOD,

AT PRICE NO MAN MAY DARE

TO LESSEN OR MISUNDERSTAND.

–HELEN HUNT JACKSON

Change Your Mind AND EXPAND YOUR WORLD

WE SERVE THE GOD WHO CREATED THE UNIVERSE . . . and motherhood. Never settle for a small view of God. He wants to do big things and new things in our lives. God wants us to be constantly increasing, to be rising to new heights. He wants to equip you for the vast responsibilities that motherhood entails. He wants to increase you in wisdom and help you make better decisions. He wants to pour out "His far and beyond favor" on you and your children (Ephesians 2:7).

But do you believe it? Or are you focused on your mothering failures and flaws and feelings of being overwhelmed and never being a good enough mom? Is your own wrong thinking keeping you from God's best?

It's time to *enlarge your vision*. To live your best life now, you must start looking at life through eyes of faith, visualizing the life you want to live. See your family prospering. See your children growing in the faith. See your marriage restored. You must conceive it and believe it is possible if you ever hope to experience it.

To conceive it, you must have an image on the inside of the life you want to live on the outside. This image has to become a part of you, in your thoughts, your conversations, deep down in your subconscious mind, in your actions, in every part of your being. If you develop an image of victory, success, health, abundance, joy, peace, and happiness, nothing on earth will be able to hold those things from you.

"See," God says, "I am doing a new thing! Now it springs up; do you not perceive it?" (Isaiah 43:19). Perhaps God is asking you this question today. "Don't you see what I want to do, and are you making room for it in your thinking?"

The truth is, if you will get in agreement with God, this can be the greatest time of your life. With God on your side, you cannot possibly lose. He can make a way when it looks as though there is no way. He can open doors that no man can shut. He can cause you to be at the right place, at the right time. He can supernaturally turn your life around.

Get rid of small-minded thinking and start thinking as God thinks. Think big. Think increase. Think abundance. Think more than enough for you and your children!

CONSIDER GOD'S WORD IN THE LIGHT OF MOTHERHOOD

"For I know the plans I have for you," declares the LORD,
"plans to prosper you and not to harm you,
plans to give you hope and a future."
JEREMIAH 29:11

No language can express the power and beauty and heroism and majesty of a mother's love. It shrinks not where man cowers, and grows stronger where man faints, and over the wastes of worldly fortune sends the radiance of its quenchless fidelity like a star in heaven.   —E. H. Chapin

BUT THE ANGEL SAID TO HER, "DO NOT BE AFRAID, MARY,
    YOU HAVE FOUND FAVOR WITH GOD. YOU WILL BE WITH
CHILD AND GIVE BIRTH TO A SON, AND YOU ARE
    TO GIVE HIM THE NAME JESUS."

                                    ~ LUKE 1:30-31

God Is on Your Side

As a woman, perhaps you've considered what the Virgin Mary must have felt like when the angel told her that she would conceive without knowing a man. In other words, God was saying it would happen through supernatural means. The power of the Most High God would come upon her and cause it to happen by His Spirit. And the reassurance given was profoundly simple: "For nothing is impossible with God" (Luke 1:37).

Similarly, God is constantly trying to plant new seeds in your heart. He's constantly trying to get you to conceive, to give up antiquated ideas, and spark new bursts of creativity within. He's trying to fill you with so much hope and expectancy that the seed will grow and bring forth a tremendous harvest.

Will you allow that seed to take root? It starts by being willing to change your thinking and start believing for something bigger. Interestingly, when Jesus wanted to encourage His followers to enlarge their visions, He reminded them, "You can't put new wine into old wineskins" (Matthew 9:17).

He was saying that you cannot have a larger life with restricted attitudes. Will you stretch your faith and vision and get rid of those old negative mind-sets that hold you back?

Get beyond the barriers of the past and expect God to do great things in your life. Start making room in your thinking for what God has in store for you and your family. You must conceive it in your heart and mind before you can receive it. The key is to believe, to let the seeds God is placing in your life to take root so they can grow. Expect God's favor, just as Mary did, to help you break out of the ruts and rise to new heights. Expect to excel in whatever you do.

This is your time for increase. You may have been sick for a long time, but this is your time to get well. You may have a child who is bound by addictions or bad habits, but this is the time to be set free. You may be struggling financially, but God is not limited to bank loans or having the right education. It can happen in spite of your past and what the critics are telling you. Will you believe?

Eliminate a barely-get-by mentality and let God's seed take root. Remember: With God, all things are possible.

CONSIDER GOD'S WORD IN THE LIGHT OF MOTHERHOOD

"It shall be done to you according to your faith."

MATTHEW 9:29 NASB

MY MOTHER PLANTED SEEDS OF FAITH
AND WATERED THEM WITH LOVE.

--ALICE GRAY

MOTHER LOVE IS THE FUEL THAT ENABLES

A NORMAL HUMAN BEING TO DO THE IMPOSSIBLE.

—MARION C. GARRETTY

Change Your Expectations

God has more in store for you! His dream for your life is so much greater than you can imagine. If God showed you everything He has in store for you, it would boggle your mind.

He is extremely interested in what you see through your "spiritual eyes." If you have a vision for victory in your life, you can rise to a new level. But as long as your gaze is on your problems instead of on your possibilities, you risk moving in the wrong direction and missing out on the great things God wants to do in and through you. It's a spiritual as well as a psychological fact: We move toward what we see in our minds.

Your life will follow your *expectations*. What you receive is directly connected to how you believe. If you dwell on positive thoughts, your life will move that direction; if you continually think negative thoughts, you will live a negative life, which will affect your relationship with your husband and children. If you expect defeat, failure, or mediocrity, your subconscious mind will make sure that you lose, fail, or sabotage every attempt to push above average. If you raise your level of expectancy, you will enlarge your vision.

It's time to quit limiting God. Remember: God is your source, and His creativity and resources are unlimited! God can give you a dream. One idea from God can forever change the course of your life. God is not limited by what you have or don't have. God can do anything, if you will simply stop limiting Him in your thinking.

Maybe you hail from a long line of divorce, failure, depression, mediocrity, and other personal or family problems. You need to say, "Enough is enough. I'm going to break out of this cycle and change my expectations. I'm going to start believing God for bigger and better things."

When God puts a dream in your heart, when He brings opportunities across your path, step out boldly in faith, expect the best, move forward with confidence, knowing that you are well able to do what God wants you to do. God wants to do a new thing in your life. But you've got to do your part and get outside that little box you've grown accustomed to. Start thinking big!

This could be the day you see your miracle.

CONSIDER GOD'S WORD IN THE LIGHT OF MOTHERHOOD

Brethren, I do not count myself to have apprehended;
but one thing I do, forgetting those things which are
behind and reaching forward to those things which are
ahead, I press toward the goal for the prize of the
upward call of God in Christ Jesus.

PHILIPPIANS 3:13–14 NKJV

One hundred years from now it will not matter what kind of car I drove, what kind of house I lived in, how much money I had in my bank account, or what my clothes looked like. But one hundred years from now the world may be a little better because I was important in the life of a child.

—Forest E. Witcraft

"MOTHER" MEANS SELFLESS DEVOTION, LIMITLESS SACRIFICE,

AND LOVE THAT PASSES UNDERSTANDING.

–UNKNOWN

THE *Favor-Minded* MOM

WHEN GOD LED THE HEBREW PEOPLE out of slavery in Egypt, the eleven-day journey to the Promised Land took forty years. God wanted them to move forward, but they wandered in the desert, going around the same mountain, time after time. They were trapped in a poor, defeated mentality, focusing on their problems, always complaining and fretting about the obstacles between them and their destiny.

No matter what you or your family has gone through in the past, no matter how many setbacks you've suffered or who or what has tried to thwart your progress, today is a new day, and God wants to do a new thing in your life. Don't let your past determine your future.

If you will change your thinking, God can change your life. You were born to win; you were born for greatness; you were created to be a champion to your children. Our God is called **El Shaddai**, "the God of more than enough." He's not "El Cheapo," the God of barely enough!

The Bible clearly states that God has crowned us with "glory and honor" (Psalm 8:5). The word **honor** could also be translated as "favor," and **favor** means "to assist, to provide with special advantages and to receive preferential treatment." In other words, God wants to assist you, to promote you, to give you advantages. But to experience more of God's favor, we must live more "favor-minded." We must expect God's special help and release our faith, knowing that God wants to assist us.

We can expect preferential treatment, not because of *who* we are, but because of *whose* we are. It is not because we are better than anybody else or that we deserve it. It is because our Father is the King of kings, and His glory and honor spill over onto us and our families. As God's children we can live with confidence and boldness, expecting good things. If we love God, He's working life to our advantage, and it will all work out for our good, although it may not always be the way we hope. No matter what does or doesn't happen, keep believing for the favor of God.

Live favor-minded. Get up each day and expect and declare it. Say, "I have the favor of God. My family has the favor of God." Don't sit back passively. You do your part, and God will do His part.

Consider God's Word in the Light of Motherhood

You have dwelt long enough on this mountain. . . .
Behold, I have set the land before you; go in and take
possession of the land which the Lord swore to your
fathers, to Abraham, to Isaac, and to Jacob, to give to
them and to their descendants after them.

Deuteronomy 1:6, 8 amp

ENLARGE THE PLACE OF YOUR TENT, AND LET THE CURTAINS OF YOUR HABITATIONS BE STRETCHED OUT; SPARE NOT; LENGTHEN YOUR CORDS AND STRENGTHEN YOUR STAKES. FOR YOU WILL SPREAD ABROAD TO THE RIGHT HAND AND TO THE LEFT.

–Isaiah 54:2-3 AMP

THE WOMAN WHO CREATES AND SUSTAINS A HOME AND UNDER

WHOSE HANDS CHILDREN GROW UP TO BE STRONG AND PURE

MEN AND WOMEN, IS A CREATOR SECOND ONLY TO GOD.

–HELEN HUNT JACKSON

THE *Power* OF AN
ATTITUDE *of* Faith

WHEN YOU ARE LIVING FAVOR-MINDED, the Bible says, God's blessings and "love chase after me every day of my life" (Psalm 23:6 THE MESSAGE). In other words, you won't be able to outrun the good things of God. Everywhere you go, things are going to change in your favor. Every time you turn around, somebody's going to want to do something good for you or someone in your family. Nothing is going to be able to keep you down.

The Bible is replete with examples of people who were in great need, but then the favor of God changed their situations. With the whole earth about to be destroyed by a flood, Noah "found favor" in the sight of God (Genesis 6:8) and built an ark to save his family, the animals, and himself. Practically starving to death, Ruth found "favor" with the owner of the grain field (Ruth 2:10), and eventually she and her mother-in-law's dire circumstances turned around, and their needs were supplied in abundance. Despite overwhelming adversity in slavery in Egypt, the "favor" of God was upon Joseph (Genesis 39:5–23), and no matter what people did to him, he continued to thrive.

If you will live with an attitude of faith, before long God's favor is going to show up, and that difficult situation will turn around to your benefit. In less than a year, the Old Testament character Job lost his family, his business, and his health. He lived in perpetual pain. But in the midst of that dark hour, Job said to God, "You have granted me life and favor" (Job 12:10 NKJV). Amazingly, Job was not delivered, healed, and set free until chapter 42! But at the very beginning, when his circumstances appeared most helpless, Job was saying, "God, I don't care what the situation looks like or how badly I feel. You are a good God. Your favor is going to turn this situation around."

No wonder God restored to Job twice what he had before! You may be in a situation with your child that looks impossible, but never give up on God. If you learn to stay in an attitude of faith and declare the favor of God instead of being discouraged and developing a sour attitude, God promises that good things will come to you. One touch of God's favor can turn everything around in you and your child's relationship.

CONSIDER GOD'S WORD IN THE LIGHT OF MOTHERHOOD

Though the fig tree may not blossom, nor fruit be on the vines; though the labor of the olive may fail, and the fields yield no food; though the flock may be cut off from the fold, and there be no herd in the stalls—yet I will rejoice in the LORD, I will joy in the God of my salvation.

HABAKKUK 3:17–18 NKJV

DEVELOP
a Healthy Self-Image

TRUE SELF-ESTEEM CAN BE BASED

ONLY ON WHAT GOD SAYS ABOUT ME—

NOT ON WHAT I THINK OR FEEL ABOUT MYSELF.

I AM WHO GOD SAYS I AM.

GOD COULD NOT BE EVERYWHERE,

THEREFORE HE MADE MOTHERS.

—JEWISH PROVERB

GOD SEES *You*
AS A *Champion*

WHEN THE ANGEL OF THE LORD APPEARED to tell Gideon how God wanted him to save the people of Israel from the Midianites, the first words spoken were, "The Lord is with you, you mighty man of [fearless] courage" (Judges 6:12 AMP). Gideon showed his true colors when he replied, "But Lord, how can I save Israel? My clan is the weakest in Manasseh, and I am the least in my family" (v. 15).

Sound familiar? So often, we sense God telling us that He has something big for us to do. But because of a poor self-image, we say, "God, I can't do that. You've got to find somebody more qualified. I don't have what it takes."

Your self-image is much like a self-portrait; it is who and what you picture yourself to be, which may or may not be an accurate reflection of who you really are. How you feel about yourself will have a tremendous impact on the mother you become, because you will probably speak, act, and react as the person you *think* you are. The truth is, you will never rise above the image you have of yourself in your mind.

It's interesting to note the difference between the way Gideon saw himself and the way God rewarded him. Although Gideon felt unqualified, full of fear, and lacking in confidence, God addressed him as a mighty man of fearless courage. Gideon felt weak; God saw him as strong and competent to lead His people into battle and victory.

God wants us to have healthy, positive self-images, to see ourselves as champions. You may feel you're failing as a mother, but that doesn't change God's image of you. You may feel unqualified, weak, and fearful, but God sees you as a victor! He created us in His image, and He is continually shaping us, conforming us to His character, helping us to become even more like the person He is.

Consequently, we must learn to love ourselves, faults and all, not because we are egotists, but because that's how our heavenly Father loves us. You can walk with confidence knowing that God loves you unconditionally. His love for you is based on what you are, not what you do. He created you as a unique individual—there has never been, nor will there ever be, another person exactly like you, and He sees you as His special masterpiece!

CONSIDER GOD'S WORD IN THE LIGHT OF MOTHERHOOD

But he said to me, "My grace is sufficient for you,
for my power is made perfect in weakness."
Therefore I will boast all the more gladly about my
weaknesses, so that Christ's power may rest on me.

2 CORINTHIANS 12:9

HOME IS THE ONE PLACE IN ALL THIS WORLD WHERE HEARTS
ARE SURE OF EACH OTHER. IT IS THE PLACE OF CONFIDENCE. IT
IS THE PLACE WHERE WE TEAR OFF THAT MASK OF GUARDED
AND SUSPICIOUS COLDNESS WHICH THE WORLD FORCES US TO
WEAR IN SELF-DEFENSE . . . IT IS QUITE SIMPLY A PLACE OF LOVE.
—FREDERICK W. ROBERTSON

My dear mother with the truthfulness of a mother's heart, ministered to all my woes, outward and inward, and even against hope kept prophesying good.

—Thomas Carlyle

BE *Strong* AND *Courageous*

Ten of the twelve Hebrew spies sent by Moses into Canaan to check out the opposition came back and said, "It is a land flowing with milk and honey, but there are giants in the land. Moses, *we were in our own sight* as grasshoppers. They're too strong. We'll never defeat them" (Numbers 13). Compared to the giants, the mental image they had of themselves was as small helpless grasshoppers. The battle was lost before it started.

Joshua and Caleb had a totally different report. "Moses, we are well able to possess the land. Yes, there are giants there, but our God is much bigger. Because of Him, *we are well able.* Let's go in at once and possess the land." Faced with the same giants, Joshua and Caleb believed God and refused to see themselves as grasshoppers. Instead, they saw themselves as God's men, led and empowered by God.

What a tremendous truth! You and I are "well able" people. Not because we are so powerful, but because our God is so powerful. He wants you to be a "can do" person, someone who is willing, ready, and "well able" to do what He commands. God loves to use ordinary people just like you and me, faults and all, to do extraordinary things. Don't focus on your weaknesses; focus on your God.

You may not feel capable in your own strength as a mother, but that's okay. God's Word states: "Now thanks be to God who always leads us in triumph in Christ" (2 Corinthians 2:14 NKJV). He expects us to live victoriously. He is not pleased when we mope around with a "poor me" attitude. When you do that, you're allowing your self-image to be shaped by nonbiblical concepts that are contrary to God's opinions of you. This sort of poor self-image will keep you from exercising your God-given gifts and authority, and it will rob you from experiencing the abundant life your heavenly Father wants you to have as a mom.

You can change the image you have of yourself. Start by agreeing with God. Remember, God sees you as strong and courageous, as a woman of great honor and valor. Quit making excuses and start stepping out in faith, doing what God has called you to do.

Keep going; keep growing. God has much more in store for you!

CONSIDER GOD'S WORD IN THE LIGHT OF MOTHERHOOD

"If the LORD is pleased with us, he will lead us into that land, a land flowing with milk and honey, and will give it to us. Only do not rebel against the LORD. And do not be afraid of the people of the land, because we will swallow them up. Their protection is gone, but the LORD is with us. Do not be afraid of them."

NUMBERS 14:8–9

NOTHING

CAN STOP THE

[MOM]

WITH THE RIGHT

MENTAL ATTITUDE.

—THOMAS JEFFERSON

THE MOMENT A CHILD IS BORN, THE MOTHER IS ALSO BORN.

SHE NEVER EXISTED BEFORE. THE WOMAN EXISTED, BUT THE

MOTHER, NEVER. A MOTHER IS SOMETHING ABSOLUTELY NEW.

—UNKNOWN

BE THE *Original* YOU

DARE TO BE HAPPY WITH WHO YOU ARE right now. Many social, physical, and emotional problems stem from the fact that people don't like themselves. They are uncomfortable with how they look, how they talk, or how they act. They don't like their personality. They are always comparing themselves with other people, wishing they were something different.

You were not created to mimic somebody else. You were created to be you. You can be happy with who God made you to be, and quit wishing you were something different. If God had wanted you to look like the perfect PTA mother, He would have made you look like her. If God had wanted you to have a different personality, He would have given you that personality. When you go around trying to be like somebody else, not only does it demean you, it steals your uniqueness.

An important factor in seeing yourself God's way is to understand your intrinsic sense of value. Your sense of value cannot be based on your successes or failures, how your children treat you, or how popular you are. It is not something we earn; indeed, we cannot earn it. God built value into us when He created us. As His unique creation, you have something to offer your family and this world that nobody else has, that nobody else can be. Your sense of value should be based solely on the fact that you are a child of the Most High God.

The Scripture says "we are God's workmanship" (Ephesians 2:10). The word *workmanship* implies that you are a "work in progress." Throughout our lives, God is continually shaping us into the people He wants us to be. The key to future success is to not be discouraged about your past or present while you are in the process of being "completed."

God doesn't want a bunch of clones. He likes variety, and you should not let people pressure you or make you feel badly about yourself because you don't fit their image of who you should be. Be an original, not a copycat. Be secure in who God made you to be and then go out and be the best mom you can be. Even if everybody else rejects you, remember, God stands before you with His arms open wide. Learn to be happy with who God made you.

CONSIDER GOD'S WORD IN THE LIGHT OF MOTHERHOOD

And I am convinced and sure of this very thing,
that He Who began a good work in you will
continue until the day of Jesus Christ [right up to the
time of His return], developing [that good work] and
perfecting and bringing it to full completion in you.

PHILIPPIANS 1:6 AMP

MY MOTHER IS A WOMAN WHO SPEAKS WITH HER LIFE.

–KESAYA E. NODA

You will find, as you look back upon your life, that the moments when you have really lived are the moments when you have done things in the spirit of love.

—Henry Drummond

Become WHAT YOU Believe

THERE IS A FASCINATING ACCOUNT of two blind men who heard that Jesus was passing by, and faith began to rise in their hearts. They must have thought, *We don't have to stay like this. There's hope for a better future.* So they began to cry out, "Have mercy on us, Son of David!" (Matthew 9:27).

When Jesus heard their cries, He posed an intriguing question, "Do you believe that I am able to do this?" (v. 28 NASB). Jesus wanted to know whether they had genuine faith. The blind men answered, "Yes, Lord; we believe." Then the Bible says, "[Jesus] touched their eyes and said, 'Become what you believe' " (THE MESSAGE). What a powerful statement about their faith! *You will become what you believe!*

So what are you believing? Are you believing to rise above your obstacles, that your family can live in health, abundance, healing, and victory? One of the most important aspects of seeing ourselves God's way involves developing a prosperous mind-set. Understand, God has already equipped you with everything you need to live a prosperous life and to fulfill your God-given destiny. He planted "seeds" inside you filled with possibilities, incredible potential, creative ideas, and dreams. But you have to start tapping into them. You've got to believe beyond a shadow of a doubt that you have what it takes.

God created you to excel, and He's given you ability, insight, talent, wisdom, and His supernatural power to do so. You don't have to figure out how God is going to solve your problems or bring it to pass. That's His responsibility. Your job is to believe. What you believe has a much greater impact on your life than what anybody else believes.

For instance, the Bible says, "We are more than conquerors through him who loved us" (Romans 8:37). It doesn't say we will become conquerors; it says we are more than conquerors **right now**. If you will start acting like it, talking like it, seeing yourself as more than a conqueror, you will live a prosperous and victorious life. Start looking through eyes of faith. You may be living in poverty at the moment, but don't ever let poverty live in you. The Bible shows that God takes pleasure in prospering His children. As His children prosper spiritually, physically, and materially, their increase brings God pleasure.

CONSIDER GOD'S WORD IN THE LIGHT OF MOTHERHOOD

Let the Lord be magnified, Who takes pleasure
in the prosperity of His servant.

PSALM 35:27 AMP

DISCOVER THE POWER
of Your Thoughts and Words

KEEP YOUR MIND SET ON THE REALITY

THAT GOD IS A MIRACLE-WORKING GOD.

START TALKING TO YOUR MOUNTAINS

ABOUT HOW BIG YOUR GOD IS!

A MOTHER'S HAPPINESS IS LIKE A BEACON,

LIGHTING UP THE FUTURE BUT REFLECTED ALSO

ON THE PAST IN THE GUISE OF FOND MEMORIES.

–HONORÉ DE BALZAC

Success Begins in the Mind

WHETHER OR NOT YOU ARE AWARE OF IT, a war is raging all around you, and the battle is for your mind. Your enemy's number-one target is the arena of your thoughts. If he can control how you think, he'll be able to control your entire life. King Solomon stated it this way: "As [a man] thinks within himself, so he is" (Proverbs 23:7 NASB).

Indeed, thoughts determine actions, attitudes, and self-image. Really, thoughts determine destiny, which is why the Bible warns us to guard our minds. Almost like a magnet, we draw in what we constantly think about. If we dwell on depressing, negative thoughts, we will be depressed and negative. If we think positive, happy, joyful thoughts, our life will reflect that and attract other upbeat, positive people. Our life follows our thoughts.

And our thoughts also affect our emotions. We will feel exactly the way we think. You cannot expect to feel happy unless you think happy thoughts. Conversely, it's impossible to remain discouraged unless you first think discouraging thoughts. So much of success and failure in life begins in our minds.

To win the victory in your mind, you can't sit back passively and expect this new person to suddenly appear. If you don't think you can be successful with your children, you never will be. When you think thoughts of mediocrity, you are destined to live an average life. But when you align your thoughts with God's thoughts and you start dwelling on the promises of His Word, when you constantly dwell on thoughts of His victory and favor, you will be propelled toward greatness, inevitably bound for increase and God's supernatural blessings.

Every day, when you first get up, set your mind for success. Choose to dwell on the promises of God's Word. Begin by agreeing with the psalmist, "This is the day the Lord has made, and I'm going to be happy. This is going to be a great day with our family." Magnify your God, and go out each day expecting good things.

CONSIDER GOD'S WORD IN THE LIGHT OF MOTHERHOOD

You will keep in perfect peace him whose mind
is steadfast, because he trusts in you.

ISAIAH 26:3

A LITTLE GIRL, ASKED WHERE HER HOME
WAS, REPLIED, "WHERE MOTHER IS."

–KEITH L. BROOKS

For when you looked into my mother's eyes you knew, as if He had told you, why God sent her into the world—it was to open the minds of all who looked to beautiful thoughts.

–Sir James M. Barrie

THINK ABOUT *Your Thinking*

LIFE IS TOUGH, and the demands on mothers can be overwhelming. We all get knocked down occasionally and get discouraged, but we need not remain there. We can choose our thoughts. Nobody can make us think a certain way. If you're not happy, nobody is forcing you to be unhappy. If you're negative and have a bad attitude toward your husband and children, nobody's coercing you to be sarcastic or sullen. You decide what you will entertain in your mind.

Simply because the enemy plants a negative, discouraging thought in your brain doesn't mean you have to nurture and help it grow. If you do, though, that thought will affect your emotions, your attitudes, and eventually your actions. You will be much more prone to discouragement and depression, and if you continue pondering that negative thought, it will sap the energy and strength right out of you.

Here's how it works practically. It is unrealistic to pretend that nothing bad ever happens to us and our family. Bad things happen to good people. Pretense is not the answer; nor is playing semantic games to make yourself sound more spiritual. If you are sick, admit it; but keep your thoughts on your Healer. If your body is tired, if your spirit is weary, fine: but focus your thoughts on the One who has promised, "Those who wait on the LORD shall renew their strength" (Isaiah 40:31 NKJV).

Jesus said, "In the world you will have tribulation; but be of good cheer, I have overcome the world" (John 16:33 NKJV). He wasn't saying that troublesome times wouldn't come; He was saying that when they do, we can choose our attitudes.

We must take responsibility for our minds and our actions. As long as we keep making excuses and blaming the family tree, our environment, past relationships with other people, our circumstances, and attributing blame to God, Satan, *anyone*, or *anything*, we will never be truly free and emotionally healthy. To a large extent, we can control our own destinies.

It's not your circumstances that have you down; your *thoughts* about your circumstances have you down. It is possible to be in one of the biggest battles for your life and still be filled with joy and peace and victory—if you simply learn how to choose the right thoughts. We can choose to believe that God is greater than our problems.

CONSIDER GOD'S WORD IN THE LIGHT OF MOTHERHOOD

Do not be anxious about anything, but in everything,
by prayer and petition, with thanksgiving, present your
requests to God. And the peace of God, which
transcends all understanding, will guard your hearts
and your minds in Christ Jesus.

PHILIPPIANS 4:6–7

MOTHER—THAT WAS THE BANK WHERE WE

DEPOSITED ALL OUR HURTS AND WORRIES.

—T. DeWitt Talmage

I REMEMBER MY MOTHER'S PRAYERS,

AND THEY HAVE ALWAYS FOLLOWED ME.

THEY HAVE CLUNG TO ME ALL MY LIFE.

—ABRAHAM LINCOLN

THE Power OF YOUR Words

Our words have tremendous power and are similar to seeds. By speaking them aloud, they are planted in our subconscious minds, take root, grow, and produce fruit of the same kind. Whether we speak positive or negative words, we will reap exactly what we sow. That's why we need to be extremely careful about what we think and say.

The Bible compares the tongue to the rudder of a huge ship (James 3:4). Although the rudder is small, it controls the ship's direction. Similarly, your tongue will control the direction of your life. You create an environment for either good or evil with your words, and you are going to have to live in that world you've created. If you're always murmuring, complaining, and talking about how bad life is in your home, you're going to live in a pretty miserable world.

However, God wants us to use our words to *change* our negative situations. Mom, there is a miracle in your mouth. If you want to change your world, start by changing your words.

I love what David did when he faced the giant Goliath. He didn't complain and say, "God, why do I always have huge problems?" He didn't dwell on the fact that Goliath was a skilled warrior and he was just a shepherd boy. Rather than focus on the magnitude of the obstacle before him, David looked Goliath right in the eyes and changed his whole atmosphere through the words he spoke aloud. He said, "You come against me with sword and spear and javelin, but I come against you in the name of the LORD Almighty" (1 Samuel 17:45).

Now, those are words of faith! He didn't merely *think* them; he didn't simply *pray* them. He spoke directly to the mountain of a man in front of him, and said, "Today I will give the carcasses of the Philistine army to the birds of the air" (v. 46). And with God's help, he did!

The Bible clearly tells us to speak to our mountains. Maybe your mountain is a sickness or a troubled relationship with your husband or a lack of communication with a wayward child. Whatever your mountain is, you must speak to that obstacle. Start calling yourself healed, happy, whole, blessed, and prosperous. Stop talking to God about how big your mountains are, and start talking to your mountains about how big your God is! God is a miracle-working God.

CONSIDER GOD'S WORD IN THE LIGHT OF MOTHERHOOD

"Truly I say to you, whoever says to this mountain, 'Be taken up and cast into the sea,' and does not doubt in his heart, but believes that what he says is going to happen, it will be granted him. Therefore I say to you, all things for which you pray and ask, believe that you have received them, and they will be granted you."

MARK 11:23–24 NASB

DEATH AND LIFE ARE IN THE POWER OF THE TONGUE,

AND THOSE WHO LOVE IT WILL EAT ITS FRUIT.

–Proverbs 18:21 NASB

ENCOURAGEMENT IS OXYGEN TO THE SOUL.

—GEORGE ADAMS

SPEAK Words of Faith

OUR WORDS ARE VITAL in bringing our dreams to pass. It's not enough to simply see it by faith or in your imagination. You have to begin speaking words of faith over your life and your family. Your words have enormous creative power. The moment you speak something out, you give birth to it. This is a spiritual principle, and it works whether what you are saying is positive or negative.

In that regard, many times we are our own worst enemies. Statements such as, "Nothing good ever happens to me," will literally prevent you from moving ahead in life. That's why you must learn to guard your tongue and speak only faith-filled words over your life—words of victory, health, and success about your life. This is one of the most important principles you can ever grab hold of. Simply put, your words can make or break you.

And whether we realize it or not, our words affect our children's future for either good or evil. We need to speak loving words of approval and acceptance, words that encourage, inspire, and motivate our family members to reach for new heights. When we do that, we speak blessings into their lives, words that carry spiritual authority much like the Old Testament patriarch's blessing of his children (Genesis 27:1–41). We are speaking abundance and increase, declaring God's favor in their lives.

But too often, we are harsh and fault-finding with our children. Our negative words will cause our children to lose the sense of value God has placed within them and can allow the enemy to bring all kinds of insecurity and inferiority into their lives.

What are you passing down to your children? It's not enough to think it; you must vocalize it. A blessing is not a blessing until it is spoken. Your children need to hear you say words such as, "I love you. I believe in you. I think you're great. There's nobody else like you." They need to hear your approval. They need to feel your love. They need your blessing.

Use your words to speak blessing over people. Bless your husband with your words. You can help set the direction for your children with your positive words. Speak words that encourage, inspire, and motivate. Start speaking those blessings today!

Consider God's Word in the Light of Motherhood

Out of the same mouth proceed blessing and cursing. My brethren, these things ought not to be so.

JAMES 3:10 NKJV

64 · YOUR BEST LIFE NOW
for Moms

LET GO
of the Past

IT'S TIME TO ALLOW YOUR EMOTIONAL WOUNDS TO HEAL.

LET GO OF YOUR EXCUSES,

AND STOP FEELING SORRY FOR YOURSELF.

IT'S TIME TO GET RID OF YOUR VICTIM MENTALITY.

[S]HE WHO IS FILLED WITH LOVE IS FILLED WITH GOD HIMSELF.

—ST. AUGUSTINE

LETTING Go

DON'T BE A PRISONER OF THE PAST. Some people are always dwelling on their disappointments. They can't understand why their prayers aren't being answered, why their loved one wasn't healed, why they were mistreated. Some people have lived so long in self-pity that it has become part of their identity. They don't realize that God wants to restore what's been stolen.

We've all had negative things happen to us. You may have gone through things that nobody deserves to experience in life—physical, verbal, sexual, or emotional abuse. Maybe you've struggled with a chronic illness or an irreparable physical problem. Maybe your dreams for your marriage or your child haven't worked out. I don't mean to minimize those difficult experiences, but if you want to live in victory, you can't let your past poison your future.

It's time to allow emotional wounds to heal, to let go of your excuses and stop feeling sorry for yourself. It's time to get rid of your victim mentality. Nobody—not even God—

ever promised that life would be fair. Quit comparing your life to someone else's, and quit dwelling on what could or should have been. Quit asking questions such as, "Why this?" or "Why that?" or "Why me?" Let go of those hurts and pains. Forgive the people who did you wrong. Forgive yourself for the mistakes you've made.

If you're not willing to let go of the old, don't expect God to do the new. If you've had some unfair things happen to you, make a decision that you're going to quit reliving those things in your memory. To constantly dwell on all the negatives and to focus on the mistakes you've made only perpetuates the problem. You will never be truly happy as long as you harbor bitterness in your heart. Instead, think on good things, things that will build you up and not tear you down, things that will encourage you and give you hope.

If you're going to go forward in life, you must quit looking backward. You may even need to forgive God. Perhaps you've been blaming Him for taking one of your loved ones. If you don't deal with it, you will wallow in self-pity. You must let go of those negative attitudes and the accompanying anger. Let it go. Today can be a new beginning.

CONSIDER GOD'S WORD IN THE LIGHT OF MOTHERHOOD

"Come to me, all you who are weary and burdened, and I will give you rest."

MATTHEW 11:28

You'll use the old rubble of past lives to build anew,

rebuild the foundations from out of your past.

You'll be known as those who can fix anything,

restore old ruins, rebuild and renovate, make

the community livable again.

—Isaiah 58:12 the message

IF WE TAKE CARE OF THE MOMENTS,

THE YEARS WILL TAKE CARE OF THEMSELVES.

—MARIA EDGEWORTH

Get Up and Get Movin'

A MAN IN JERUSALEM had been crippled for thirty-eight years. He spent every day lying by the pool of Bethesda, hoping for a miracle (John 5). This man had a deep-seated, lingering disorder similar to what many people have today. Their maladies may not be physical; they may be emotional, but they are deep-seated, lingering disorders nonetheless. They may stem from unforgiveness or holding on to past resentments, and they affect your personality, your relationships, and your self-image. Some people sit back for years, waiting for a miracle to happen that will make everything better.

When Jesus saw the man lying there, He asked a simple, straightforward question: "Do you want to be made well?" The man's response was interesting. He began listing all of his excuses. "I'm all alone. I don't have anyone to help me." Is it any wonder that he had not been healed?

Jesus looked at him and said, in effect, "If you are serious about getting well, if you want to get out of this mess, get up off the ground, take up your bed, and be on your way." When the man did what Jesus told him to do, he was miraculously healed!

If you're serious about being well, you can't lie around feeling sorry for yourself. Don't waste another minute trying to figure out why certain evil things have happened to you or your loved ones. You may never know the answer. But don't use that as an excuse to wallow in self-pity. Leave it alone, get up, and move on with your life. Trust God and accept the fact that there will be some unanswered questions. Just because you don't know the answer doesn't mean that one does not exist.

Each of us should have what I call an "I Don't Understand It" file. When something comes up for which you have no reasonable answer, instead of dwelling on the "why," simply place it in this file and don't become bitter. Trust God, get up, walk out of any emotional bondage in which you have been living, and step into the great future He has for you. If you will stay in an attitude of faith and victory, God has promised that He will turn those emotional wounds around. He'll use them to your advantage, and you will come out better than you would have had they not happened to you.

CONSIDER GOD'S WORD IN THE LIGHT OF MOTHERHOOD

Let us also lay aside every encumbrance and the sin
which so easily entangles us, and let us run with
endurance the race that is set before us.

HEBREWS 12:1 NASB

LIFE IS SHORT AND WE NEVER HAVE ENOUGH TIME FOR
GLADDENING THE HEARTS OF THOSE WHO TRAVEL THE WAY
WITH US. O, BE SWIFT TO LOVE! MAKE HASTE TO BE KIND.

—HENRI FREDERICK AMIEL

"FOR IF YOU FORGIVE MEN WHEN THEY SIN AGAINST YOU,

YOUR HEAVENLY FATHER WILL ALSO FORGIVE YOU.

BUT IF YOU DO NOT FORGIVE MEN THEIR SINS,

YOUR FATHER WILL NOT FORGIVE YOUR SINS."

–MATTHEW 6:14–15

Forgive to Be Free

Many people are trying to improve their lives by dealing with the external aspects. They are attempting to rectify their bad habits, bad attitudes, bad tempers, or negative and sour personalities. Trying to change the fruit of their lives is noble, but unless they get to the root, they will never change the fruit—the problems will persist. You may be able to control your behavior or keep a good attitude for a while, but you can't be free.

You have to go deeper. Many people attempt to bury the hurt and pain in their hearts or their subconscious minds. They don't realize it, but much of their inner turmoil is because their own heart is poisoned. The Bible says, "Keep thy heart with all diligence; for out of it are the issues of life" (Proverbs 4:23 KJV). In other words, if we have bitterness on the inside, it will contaminate our personalities and our attitudes, as well as how we treat our children and husbands.

If you want to live your best life now, you must be quick to forgive. You need to forgive so you can be free, out of bondage, and happy. When we forgive, we're not doing it just for the other person, we're doing it for our own good.

When we hold on to unforgiveness and live with grudges, all we're doing is building walls of separation. We think we're protecting ourselves, but we're not. We are simply shutting other people out of our lives. We become isolated, alone, warped, and imprisoned by our own bitterness, and it can happen right inside our family life.

Do you realize that those walls also prevent God's blessings from pouring into your life? Those walls can stop the flow of God's favor and keep your prayers from being answered. They'll keep your dreams from coming to pass. You must tear down the walls. You must forgive the people who hurt you so you can get out of prison. You'll never be free until you do. Let go of those wrongs they've done to you. Get that bitterness out of your life. That's the only way you're going to truly be free.

You may experience genuine physical and emotional healing as you search your heart and are willing to forgive. You may see God's favor in a fresh, new way. You'll be amazed at what can happen when you release all that poison.

CONSIDER GOD'S WORD IN THE LIGHT OF MOTHERHOOD

See to it that no one misses the grace of God
and that no bitter root grows up
to cause trouble and defile many.

HEBREWS 12:15

THE HEART OF A MOTHER IS A DEEP ABYSS AT THE

BOTTOM OF WHICH YOU ALWAYS FIND FORGIVENESS.

—HONORÉ DE BALZAC

I WANT TO BE LIKE YOU—A WELL-WATERED GARDEN WHOSE

FRAGRANCE CAUSES ALL AROUND TO BREATHE IN . . . DEEPLY.

—KIMBER ANNIE ENGSTROM

KEEP MOVING *Forward*

ONE OF THE MOST IMPORTANT KEYS to moving forward into the great future God has for you is learning how to overcome the disappointments in your life. Because disappointments can pose such formidable obstacles to letting go of the past, you need to be sure you have dealt with this area before taking the next step to living at your full potential.

Often, defeating disappointments and letting go of the past are the flip side of the same coin, especially when you are disappointed in yourself. When you do something wrong, don't hold on to it and beat yourself up about it. Admit it, seek forgiveness, and move on. Be quick to let go of your mistakes and failures, hurts, pains, and sins.

Being lied to by a child, betrayed by a husband, walked out on by a loved one—certainly, these kinds of losses leave indelible scars, causing you to want to hold on to your grief. It would be logical for you to seek revenge. Many people would even encourage you to do so.

But that is not God's plan for you. God has promised that if you will put your trust in Him to bring about the justice in your life, He will pay you back for all the unfair things that have happened to you (Isaiah 61:7–9). That means you don't have to go around trying to pay everybody back for the wrong things they have done to you. God is your vindicator. Let Him fight your battles for you. Turn matters over to Him and let Him handle them His way.

When you suffer loss, nobody expects you to be an impenetrable rock. When we experience failure or loss, it's natural to feel remorse or sorrow. That's the way God made us. But you must make a decision that you are going to move on. It won't happen automatically. You will have to rise up and say, "I don't care how hard this is, I am not going to let this get the best of me."

Don't live in regret or remorse or sorrow. They will only interfere with your faith. Faith must always be a present-tense reality, not a distant memory. God will turn those disappointments around. He will take your scars and turn them into stars for His glory.

CONSIDER GOD'S WORD IN THE LIGHT OF MOTHERHOOD

Beloved, never avenge yourselves, but leave the way open for [God's] wrath; for it is written, Vengeance is Mine, I will repay (requite), says the Lord.

ROMANS 12:19 AMP

FIND STRENGTH
Through Adversity

GOD HAS A DIVINE PURPOSE

FOR EVERY CHALLENGE

THAT COMES INTO OUR LIVES.

TRIALS TEST OUR CHARACTER

AND HELP SHAPE OUR FAITH.

WHAT DO YOU THINK ABOUT WHEN YOU THINK ABOUT LOVE?

MOTHER'S LOVE, THE LOVE OF CHILDREN—

WHICH IS SO BEAUTIFUL, SO STRONG, SO JOYFUL.

—KIM PHUC

Get Up ON THE INSIDE

LIVING YOUR BEST LIFE NOW is downright difficult sometimes. Many of us give up far too easily when things don't go our way or we face adversity. Instead of persevering, we get all bent out of shape. Before long we're down and discouraged, which is understandable, especially when we've struggled with a family problem or a weakness for a long time. Eventually we acquiesce.

But we have to be more determined than that. Our circumstances in life may occasionally knock us down, but we must not stay down. Even if you can't see up on the outside, get up on the inside. Have that victor's attitude and mentality. Stay with an attitude of faith.

To live your best life now, you must act on your will, not simply your emotions. Sometimes that means you have to take steps of faith even when you are hurting, grieving, or still reeling from an attack of the enemy. Before David became king of Israel, he and his men returned home to find their homes burned, their possessions stolen, and their women and children kidnapped. Instead of sitting around devastated and mourning over what had been lost, David encouraged himself in the Lord and convinced his men to attack the enemy (1 Samuel 30:6). As they persevered, God supernaturally helped them to recover everything that had been stolen.

You may be sitting around waiting for God to change your husband's behavior or your child's attitude. *Then* you're going to be happy; *then* you're going to have a good attitude; *then* you're going to give God praise. But God is waiting for you to get up on the inside as David did. It will take courage; it will definitely take determination, but you can do it if you decide to do so.

Develop a victor's mentality and watch what God begins to do. Set your face like a flint and say, "God, I may not understand this, but I know You are still in control. And You said all things would work together for my good. You said You would take this evil and turn it around and use it to my advantage. So, Father, I thank You that You are going to bring me through this!" No matter what you may face in life, if you know how to get up on the inside, adversities cannot keep you down.

CONSIDER GOD'S WORD IN THE LIGHT OF MOTHERHOOD

Use every piece of God's armor to resist the enemy
in the time of evil, so that after the battle you
will still be standing firm.

EPHESIANS 6:13 NLT

[LOVE] ALWAYS PROTECTS, ALWAYS TRUSTS,

ALWAYS HOPES, AND ALWAYS PERSEVERES.

—1 CORINTHIANS 13:7

THE MOST GLORIOUS SIGHT THAT ONE EVER SEES BENEATH

THE STARS IS THE SIGHT OF WORTHY MOTHERHOOD.

–GEORGE W. TRUETT

TRUST God's Timing

When many people face adversity, they allow their doubt to cloud their determination, thus weakening their faith. They don't keep a good attitude. But life is too short to trudge through it depressed and defeated. No matter what has come against you or what is causing you to slip and fall, no matter who or what is trying to push you down, you need to keep getting up on the inside and learn to be happy.

Medical science tells us that people with a determined, feisty spirit get well quicker than people who are prone to be negative and discouraged. That's because God made us to be determined, not to live in depression and defeat. A negative spirit dries up your energy; it weakens your immune system. Many people are living with physical ailments and emotional bondages because they are not standing up on the inside.

It is our nature to want everything to be right now. When we pray for our dreams to come to pass or for an adversity to pass, we want answers immediately. But we have to understand, God has an appointed time to answer our prayers. And the truth is, no matter how badly we want it sooner, it's not going to change His appointed time.

When we misunderstand God's timing, we live upset and frustrated, wondering when God is going to do something. But when you understand God's timing, you won't live all stressed out. You can relax knowing that God is in control of you and your family, and at the "appointed time" He is going to make it happen. It may be next week, next year, or ten years from now. But whenever it is, you can rest assured it will be in God's timing.

God is not like an ATM machine, where you punch in the right prayer codes and receive what you requested within twenty-four hours. No, we all have to wait and learn to trust God. The key is, are we going to wait with a good attitude and expectancy, knowing God is at work whether we can see anything happening or not? We need to know that behind the scenes, God is putting all the pieces together. And one day, at the appointed time, you will see the culmination of everything that God has been doing. God often works the most when we see it and feel it the least.

CONSIDER GOD'S WORD IN THE LIGHT OF MOTHERHOOD

For the vision is yet for an appointed time; but at the end it will speak, and it will not lie. Though it tarries, wait for it; because it will surely come, it will not tarry.

HABAKKUK 2:3 NKJV

THE MOTHER'S HEART IS THE CHILD'S SCHOOLROOM.

–HENRY WARD BEECHER

"For my thoughts are not your thoughts, neither are

your ways my ways," declares the Lord. "As the heavens

are higher than the earth, so are my ways higher than

your ways and my thoughts than your thoughts."

—Isaiah 55:8–9

BE Content

DAVID HAD A BIG DREAM FOR HIS LIFE. He had a desire to make a difference, but as a young man he spent many years as a shepherd, caring for his father's sheep. I'm sure there were plenty of times when he must have thought, *God, what am I doing here? There's no future in this place. When are You going to change this situation?* But David understood God's timing. He knew that if he would be faithful in obscurity, God would promote him at the right time. He knew God would bring his dreams to pass in due season.

You know the story. God brought David out of those fields, he defeated Goliath, and eventually he was made king of Israel.

Perhaps you have a big dream in your heart—a dream to have a better marriage, to own your own business, to help hurting people—but like David, you don't really see any human way your dream could happen.

We don't always understand God's methods. His ways don't always make sense to us, but we have to realize that God sees the big picture. God isn't limited to natural, human ways of doing things. Consider this possibility: You may be ready for what God has for you, but your child, who is going to be involved, is not ready yet. God has to do a work in your child or another situation before your prayer can be answered according to God's will for your life. All the pieces have to come together for it to be God's perfect time.

But never fear; God is getting everything lined up in your life. You may not feel it; you may not see it. Your situation may look just as it did for the past ten years, but then one day, in a split second of time, God will bring it all together. When it is God's timing, all the forces of darkness can't stop Him. When it's your due season, God will bring it to pass.

Don't grow impatient and try to force doors to open. Don't try to make things happen in your own strength. Contentment starts in your attitude. The answer will come, and it will be right on time. He will bring your dreams to pass. Rest in Him! Let God do it His way.

CONSIDER GOD'S WORD IN THE LIGHT OF MOTHERHOOD

But I trust in you, O LORD; I say, "You are my God."
My times are in your hands.

PSALM 31:14–15

OUR GREATEST DANGER IN LIFE IS IN PERMITTING
THE URGENT THINGS TO CROWD OUT THE IMPORTANT.

−CHARLES E. HUMMEL

My mother had a slender, small body, but a large heart—a heart so large that everybody's joys found welcome in it, and hospitable accommodation.

—Mark Twain

TESTS OF *Faith*

WHEN ADVERSITY COMES KNOCKING AT THE DOOR or calamities occur within a family, some moms immediately think they have done something wrong, that God surely must be punishing them. They don't understand that God has a divine purpose for every challenge that comes into our lives. He doesn't send problems, but sometimes He allows us to go through them.

Why is that? The Bible says temptations, trials, and difficulties must come, because if we are to strengthen our spiritual muscles and grow stronger, we must have adversities to overcome and attacks to resist. Trials are intended to test our character, to test our faith. If you will learn to cooperate with God and be quick to change and correct the areas He brings to light, then you'll pass that test and be promoted to a new level.

In the Bible, we read of Job, a good man who loved God and had a heart to do what's right. Yet in a few weeks' time, he lost his business, his flocks and herds, his family, and his health. Things could not get any worse for Job, and I'm sure he was tempted to be bitter. His own wife told him, "Curse God and die."

But no, Job knew that God is a God of restoration. He knew God could turn any situation around. And his attitude was, *Even if I die I'm going to die trusting God. I'm going to die believing for the best.* Sustaining faith is what got Job through those dark nights of the soul when he didn't know where to go or what to do . . . but because of his faith in God, he did. And, when it was all said and done, God not only turned Job's calamity around, He brought Job out with twice that he had before.

God often allows you to go through difficult situations to draw out those impurities in your character. You can pray and resist it, but it's not going to do any good. God is more interested in changing you than He is in changing the circumstances. You may not always like it; you may want to run from it; you may even resist it, but God is going to keep bringing up the issue again and again until you pass the test. Faith tells you the best is yet to come.

CONSIDER GOD'S WORD IN THE LIGHT OF MOTHERHOOD

Beloved, do not be surprised at the fiery ordeal
among you, which comes upon you for your testing,
as though some strange thing were happening to you.

1 PETER 4:12 NASB

LIVE
to Give

GOD IS A GIVER,

AND IF YOU WANT HIM TO POUR OUT

HIS BLESSING AND FAVOR IN YOUR LIFE,

THEN YOU MUST LEARN TO BE

A GIVER AND NOT A TAKER.

I CANNOT FORGET MY MOTHER. SHE IS MY BRIDGE.

WHEN I NEEDED TO GET ACROSS, SHE STEADIED

HERSELF LONG ENOUGH FOR ME TO RUN ACROSS SAFELY.

—RENITA WEEMS

No "Lone Ranger" Moms

MANY PEOPLE NOWADAYS ARE blatantly and unashamedly living for themselves. Society teaches us to look out for number one. "What's in it for me?" We readily acknowledge this as the "me" generation, and that same narcissism sometimes spills over into our relationship with God, our families, and one another. Ironically, this selfish attitude condemns us to living shallow, unrewarding lives. No matter how much we acquire for ourselves, we are never satisfied.

One of the greatest challenges we face in our quest to enjoy our best lives now is the temptation to live selfishly. Because we believe that God wants the best for us, and that He wants us to prosper, it is easy to slip into the subtle trap of selfishness. Not only will you avoid that pitfall, but you will have more joy than you dreamed possible when you live to give, which is the sixth step to living at your full potential.

God is a giver, and if you want to experience a new level of God's joy, if you want Him to pour out His blessing and favor in your life, then you must learn to be a giver and not a taker. We were not made to function as self-involved people, thinking only of ourselves. No, God created us to be givers. And you will never be truly fulfilled as a human being until you learn the simple secret of how to give your life away.

The spiritual principle is that when we reach out to other people in need, God will make sure that your own needs are supplied. If you want your dreams to come to pass, help someone else fulfill his or her dreams. If you're down and discouraged, get your mind off yourself and go help meet your child's need. Sow the seed that will bring you a harvest.

Perhaps you feel you have nothing to give. Sure you do! You can give a smile or a hug. You can do some menial but meaningful task to help someone. You can visit someone in the hospital or make a meal for a person who is shut in. You can write an encouraging letter. Your child needs what you have to share. Your husband needs your love and friendship. God created us to be free, but He didn't make us to function as "Lone Ranger" moms. We need one another.

———————————

CONSIDER GOD'S WORD IN THE LIGHT OF MOTHERHOOD

Remember the words of the Lord Jesus, how he said,
It is more blessed to give than to receive.

ACTS 20:35 KJV

THE ONE THING WE NEVER GIVE ENOUGH OF IS LOVE.

–HENRY MILLER

THE ANGELS, WHISPERING TO ONE ANOTHER, CAN FIND

AMONG THEIR BURNING TERMS OF LOVE, NONE

SO DEVOTIONAL AS THAT OF MOTHER.

—EDGAR ALLAN POE

WALK in Love

If anybody had a right to return evil instead of love, it was Joseph. His brothers hated him so much, they purposed to kill him but then sold him into slavery. Years went by, and Joseph experienced all sorts of troubles and heartaches. But Joseph kept a good attitude, and God continued to bless him. After thirteen years of being in prison for a crime he didn't commit, God supernaturally promoted him to the second highest position in Egypt.

When Joseph's brothers came to Egypt and suddenly found their lives were in Joseph's hands, can you imagine the fear that gripped their hearts? This was Joseph's opportunity to pay them back. Yet Joseph extended his mercy. Is it any wonder he was so blessed with God's favor? Joseph knew how to treat people right.

How you treat other people can have a great impact on the degree of blessings and favor of God you will experience in your life. You may have children who have done you great wrong. You may feel as though your whole life has been stolen away by somebody. But if you will choose to forgive them, you can overcome that evil with good. You can get to the point where you can look at the people who have hurt you and return good for evil. If you do that, God will pour out His favor in your life in a fresh way. He will honor you; He will reward you, and He'll make those wrongs right.

The Bible says we are to "aim to show kindness and seek to do good" (1 Thessalonians 5:15 AMP). We must be proactive. We should be on the lookout to share His mercy, kindness, and goodness with people. Moreover, we need to be kind and do good to people even when somebody is unkind to us, including our children. The last thing they need is for you to respond angrily.

Keep taking the high road and be kind and courteous. Walk in love and have a good attitude. God sees what you're doing, and He is our vindicator. He will make sure your good actions and attitude will overcome that evil. If you'll keep doing the right thing, you will come out far ahead of where you would have been had you fought fire with fire. God wants His people to help heal wounded hearts.

CONSIDER GOD'S WORD IN THE LIGHT OF MOTHERHOOD

Love (God's love in us) does not insist on its own rights or its own way, for it is not self-seeking; it is not touchy or fretful or resentful; it takes no account of the evil done to it [it pays no attention to a suffered wrong].

1 CORINTHIANS 13:5 AMP

"You meant evil against me, but God meant it for good in order to bring about this present result, to preserve many people alive."

—Genesis 50:20 NASB

A MOTHER IS SOMEONE WHO DREAMS FOR YOU,

BUT THEN LETS YOU CHASE THE DREAMS YOU

HAVE FOR YOURSELF AND LOVES YOU JUST THE SAME.

–Unknown

Keep an *Open Heart*

Everywhere you go these days people are hurting and discouraged; many have broken dreams. They've made mistakes; their lives are in a mess. They need to feel God's compassion and His unconditional love. They don't need somebody to judge and criticize them. They need somebody to bring hope, to bring healing, to show God's mercy. Really, they are looking for a friend, somebody who will be there to encourage them, who will take the time to listen to their story and genuinely care.

Our world is crying out for people with compassion, people who love unconditionally, people who will take some time to help. Certainly, when God created us, He put His supernatural love in all of our hearts. He's placed in you the potential to have a kind, caring, gentle, loving spirit. Because you are created in God's image, you have the moral capacity to experience God's compassion in your heart.

If you study the life of Jesus, you will discover that He always took time for people. He was never too busy with His own agenda, with His own plans. He wasn't so caught up in

Himself that He was unwilling to stop and help a person in need. He could have easily said, "Listen, I'm busy. I have a schedule to keep." But no, Jesus had compassion on people. He was concerned about what they were going through, and He willingly took time to meet their needs. He freely gave of His life.

If you want to live your best life now, you must make sure that you keep your heart of compassion open. We need to be willing to be interrupted and inconvenienced if it means we can help meet our children's needs. Sometimes if we would just take the time to listen to our child, we could help initiate a healing process in his or her life. If you can open your heart of compassion—without judging or condemning—and simply have an ear to listen, you have the opportunity to make a difference in your child's life.

Learn to follow the flow of God's divine love. Don't ignore it. Act on it. Your child needs what you have.

CONSIDER GOD'S WORD IN THE LIGHT OF MOTHERHOOD

If anyone . . . sees his brother and fellow believer
in need, yet closes his heart of compassion against him,
how can the love of God live and remain in him?

1 JOHN 3:17 AMP

THE SUPREME HAPPINESS OF LIFE IS THE CONVICTION

THAT WE ARE LOVED; LOVED FOR OURSELVES.

—VICTOR HUGO

WHOEVER SOWS SPARINGLY WILL ALSO REAP SPARINGLY,

AND WHOEVER SOWS GENEROUSLY WILL ALSO REAP

GENEROUSLY. EACH MAN SHOULD GIVE WHAT HE HAS

DECIDED IN HIS HEART TO GIVE, NOT RELUCTANTLY OR

UNDER COMPULSION, FOR GOD LOVES A CHEERFUL GIVER.

–2 CORINTHIANS 9:6–7

God Loves a Cheerful Giver

Don't let anybody convince you that it doesn't make any difference whether you give. In the Bible, a Roman named Cornelius and his family became the first recorded Gentile household to experience salvation after the resurrection of Jesus. Why was Cornelius chosen for this honor? Cornelius was told in a vision: "Your prayers and charities have not gone unnoticed by God!" (Acts 10:4 TLB). I'm not suggesting that you can buy miracles or that you have to pay God to meet your needs. But I am saying that God sees your gifts and acts of kindness. It pleases God when you give, and He will pour out His favor on you.

All through the Bible, we find the principle of sowing and reaping. "Whatever a man sows, that he will also reap" (Galatians 6:7 NKJV). Just as a farmer must plant some seed if he hopes to reap a harvest, we, too, must plant some good seed in the fields of our families, careers, and personal relationships. If you want to reap happiness, you have to sow some "happiness" seeds by making others happy. If you want to reap financial blessing, you must sow financial seeds in the lives of others. The seed always has to lead.

In the midst of a great famine in the land of Canaan, Isaac did something that people without insight may have thought rather odd. He sowed seed and then reaped a hundredfold crop, because the Lord blessed him (Genesis 26:12). In his time of need, Isaac didn't wait around, expecting someone else to come to his rescue. No, he acted in faith, and God supernaturally multiplied that seed.

God is keeping a record of every good deed you've ever done, including ones within your family. You may think it went unnoticed, but God saw it. And in your time of need, He will make sure that somebody is there to help you. Your generous gifts will come back to you. God has seen every smile you've ever given to a hurting child. He's observed every time you went out of the way to lend a helping hand. God has witnessed when you have given sacrificially, even giving money to others that perhaps you needed desperately for yourself or your family. God has promised that your generous gifts will come back to you (see Luke 6:38). When you are generous to others, God will always be generous with you.

———————————————

CONSIDER GOD'S WORD IN THE LIGHT OF MOTHERHOOD

A generous man will prosper; he who refreshes
others will himself be refreshed.

PROVERBS 11:25

CHOOSE
to Be Happy

LEARN TO LIVE ONE DAY AT A TIME.

BY AN ACT OF YOUR WILL, CHOOSE TO

START ENJOYING YOUR LIFE RIGHT NOW.

ENJOY EVERYTHING IN YOUR LIFE.

A MOTHER LAUGHS OUR LAUGHS, SHEDS OUR TEARS, RETURNS

OUR LOVE, FEARS OUR FEARS. SHE LIVES OUR JOYS, CARES OUR

CARES, AND ALL OUR HOPES AND DREAMS SHE SHARES.

—JULIA SUMMERS

Happiness IS YOUR CHOICE

THE APOSTLE PAUL WROTE MORE THAN HALF of the New Testament while incarcerated, often in prison cells not much bigger than a small bathroom. Yet Paul wrote such amazing faith-filled words as, "I can do all things through Christ who strengthens me" (Philippians 4:13 NKJV). And, "Thanks be to God, who always causes us to triumph," and "Rejoice in the Lord always" (Philippians 4:4 NKJV). Notice that we are to rejoice and be happy at all times. In your difficulties, when things aren't going well with your children, make a decision to stay full of joy.

You need to understand that the enemy is not really after your dreams, your health, or your finances. He's not primarily after your family. He's after your joy. The Bible says that "the joy of the LORD is your strength" (Nehemiah 8:10 NKJV), and your enemy knows if he can deceive you into living down in the dumps and depressed, then you are not going to have the necessary strength—physically, emotionally, or spiritually—to withstand his attacks.

It is a simple yet profound truth: Happiness is a choice. You don't have to wait for everything to be perfect in your family. You don't have to forgo happiness until you lose weight, break an unhealthy habit, or accomplish all your goals. The seventh step to enjoying your best life now is to choose to be happy today.

You might as well choose to be happy and enjoy your life! When you do that, not only will you feel better, but your faith will cause God to show up and work wonders. To do so, you must learn to live one day at a time; better yet, make the most of this moment. It's good to set goals and make plans, but if you're always living in the future, you're never really enjoying the present in the way God wants us to.

We need to understand that God gives us the grace to live today. He has not yet given us tomorrow's grace, and we should not worry about it. By an act of your will, choose to start enjoying your life right now. Learn how to smile and laugh. Quit being so uptight and stressed out. Enjoy your family, friends, and health; enjoy everything in your life. Happiness is a decision you make, not an emotion you feel. Happiness is your choice.

CONSIDER GOD'S WORD IN THE LIGHT OF MOTHERHOOD

A cheerful heart is good medicine, but a
crushed spirit dries up the bones.

PROVERBS 17:22

IT ISN'T THE BIG PLEASURES THAT COUNT THE MOST;

IT IS MAKING A GREAT DEAL OUT OF THE LITTLE ONES.

—UNKNOWN

When you thought I wasn't looking, I heard you
say a prayer, and I believed there is a God I could
always talk to. . . . When you thought I wasn't
looking, I saw that you cared, and I wanted to
be everything that I could be.

—Mary Rita Schilke Korzan

BE A PERSON OF
Excellence AND Integrity

FOR MANY MOMS, MEDIOCRITY IS THE NORM; they want to do as little as they possibly can and still get by. But God did not create us to be mediocre. He doesn't want us to just barely get by. God has called us to be people of excellence and integrity, people of honor, people who are trustworthy. Indeed, the only way to be truly happy is to live with excellence and integrity. Any hint of compromise will taint our greatest victories or our grandest achievements.

A person of excellence goes the extra mile to do what's right. A person of integrity is open and honest and true to her word. She doesn't have any hidden agendas or ulterior motives. People of excellence give their employers a full day's work; they don't come in late, leave early, or call in sick when they are not. When you have an excellent spirit, it shows up in the quality of your housework, and the attitude with which you do it. People of integrity are the same in private as they are in public. They do what's right whether anybody is watching or not.

If you don't have integrity, you will never reach your highest potential. Integrity is the foundation on which a truly successful life is built. Every time you compromise, every time you are less than honest, you are causing a slight crack in the foundation. If you continue compromising, that foundation will never be able to hold what God wants to build. You'll never have lasting prosperity if you don't first have integrity. You may enjoy some temporary success, but you'll never see the fullness of God's favor if you don't take the high road and make the more excellent choices. On the other hand, God's blessings will overtake us if we settle for nothing less than living with integrity.

God's people are people of excellence. Remember: You represent Almighty God. How you live, how you care for your children and do your work, is all a reflection on our God. If you want to live your best life now, start aiming for excellence in everything you do. Whatever we do, we should give our best effort and do it as if we were doing it for God. If we'll work with that standard in mind, God promises to reward us, and others will be attracted to our God.

———————————————

CONSIDER GOD'S WORD IN THE LIGHT OF MOTHERHOOD

"Whoever can be trusted with very little can also be
trusted with much, and whoever is dishonest with
very little will also be dishonest with much."

LUKE 16:10

THE FUTURE DESTINY OF A CHILD IS ALWAYS

THE WORK OF A MOTHER.

–NAPOLEON

A MOTHER IS THE TRUEST FRIEND WE HAVE, WHEN TRIALS HEAVY AND

SUDDEN, FALL UPON US; WHEN ADVERSITY TAKES THE PLACE OF PROSPERITY;

WHEN FRIENDS WHO REJOICE WITH US IN OUR SUNSHINE DESERT US; WHEN

TROUBLE THICKENS AROUND US, STILL WILL SHE CLING TO US, AND

ENDEAVOR BY HER KIND PRECEPTS AND COUNSELS TO DISSIPATE THE

CLOUDS OF DARKNESS, AND CAUSE PEACE TO RETURN TO OUR HEARTS.

—WASHINGTON IRVING

YOUR *Best Life* NOW

GOD'S MOMS SHOULD BE THE HAPPIEST MOMS ON EARTH! So happy, in fact, that other people notice. Living your best life now is living with enthusiasm and being excited about the life God has given you. It is believing for more good things in the days ahead, but it is also living in the moment and enjoying it to the hilt!

Let's not be naïve. The pressures, tensions, and stress of modern life constantly threaten to take a toll on our enthusiasm. You probably know some people who have lost their passion and zest for life. One of the main reasons we lose our enthusiasm in life is because we start to take for granted what God has done for us. We get accustomed to His goodness; it becomes routine.

Don't take for granted the greatest gift of all that God has given you—Himself! Don't allow your relationship with Him to become stale or your appreciation for His goodness to become common. We need to stir ourselves up, to replenish our supply of God's good gifts on a daily basis. Our lives need to be inspired, infused, filled afresh with His goodness every day.

Don't just go through the motions in life. Make a decision that you are not going to live another day without the joy of the Lord in your life; without love, peace, and passion; without being excited about your life. And understand that you don't have to have something extraordinary happening in your life to be excited. You may not have the perfect children or the perfect marriage or live in the perfect home, but you can still choose to live each day aglow with God's presence.

If you want to see God's favor, do everything with your whole heart. Do it with passion and some fire. Not only will you feel better, but that fire will spread, and soon other people will want what you have. Wherever you are in life, make the most of it and be the best you can be.

Raise your level of expectancy. It's our faith that activates the power of God. Let's quit limiting Him with our small-minded thinking and start believing Him for bigger and better things. God will take you places you've never dreamed of, and you will be having your best life now.

CONSIDER GOD'S WORD IN THE LIGHT OF MOTHERHOOD

Never lag in zeal and in earnest endeavor; be aglow
and burning with the Spirit, serving the Lord.

ROMANS 12:11 AMP

JOY IS A NET OF LOVE BY WHICH YOU CAN CATCH SOULS.

—MOTHER TERESA